Seeking the Mystical Theory of Everything

Lucas Klesch

Sunshine Ink

Cover Design by The Fresch Klesch
@TheFreschKlesch
www.freschklesch.com

Photographs in cover design are courtesy of NASA.

This book is dedicated to the idea we are
connected to each other on a quantum level,
and this is how our love spreads throughout all
spacetime.

All book and publishing inquiries should
be sent to:
studiogallery@sunshineink.us

Stay connected with Sunshine Ink at:
www.sunshineink.us
@SunshineInk1975

Chapters   Page

entropy wins
always

today the weight
of my specific gravity
feels like it will crush
my blue core
the early spring sky
of these dying days
a dream abandoned
to entrepreneurial capitalism
the planet in climate crisis
a species ending existence
due to the greed
of a self centered populace
if this is the end
could i spend it with you

the clarity of turmoil
occurs upon acceptance
when we long for
the simplicity of knowing
why our heart weeps
on days we lack sleep
the anxiety of the morning
comes from dream residuals
we did not wash away
while enjoying our coffee
failures like this are systemic
when your capacity is low
the cadence laughs
like there is no tomorrow
we can use our divinity for
quantum communications
encrypted messages
for our shared future
i have the mathematics
of shear will
to manifest a future
i perpetually dream about
i saw myself in a dive
all those productive years
wasted in the din
of neon lottery
isolated in the dark
i pissed away
a thousand opportunities
gambling productivity

i am neither
rich or poor
i am stuck
between
perpetual
fabrication
and real
freedom

i will fuse the space
between us
with super charged
particles of joy
these gluons of love
bind us with ferocity
when we follow
the motion of
brownian wanderlust

the sinister moment of panic
burned away under threat
of sunshine and success
the day cascaded
all this hope
of a fixed moment
in spatial time
a universal coordinate
i worked the muscles
to acceptance
until they vibrated
delicately
with the faith required
of pursuing something
more than yourself

all those dollars
felt as much
like extortion
as a dowlry
the sum of
a singular totality
creating
a way forward

the memory of
your skin
lingers
all the days
since
i floated away
with all the
regret and
a belief
i could not
leap
your way
without
recovering
first

you smiled
after we kissed
in that spring
night
when we
stopped traffic
it fills
my heart
to this day
feeling
our savage
kisses
our bodies seeking
respite
joy
pleasure

all my memories
faded
i was broken
one hundred seventy
degrees from center
it took me
years
to reconcile
the geometric means
hiding vague
memories
of love

vibrational love poems
jazz the emotional
rollercoaster
these melancholy
notes are wildflowers
in bloom
strewn
to the wind
wanderlust
craves more than
oxygen
blowing
out the sun

i linger with a brilliant hue
on long days that end
when the skyline fades
from pink to purple
it tastes like you
when i sniff this alone
inhaling all the
nostalgia left behind
by the chemistry
of a charge transfer
of symbolic memory

the dry old hardwoods
sing a moist song of history
the trashy side of delta
living with a melodic tune
of moonshine follies
we shared a meal
then some whiskey
as i wrote a book
of poetry in my head
on the way home

the clarity of this blue sky
mixed fluffy grey clouds
thinned by tropospheric mixing
my need for this
is only surpassed by my
need to feel you
the vitamin k will be your surrogate
until i have the energy
to quantum tunnel
to you one day
i hope
the math
is functional
for one of us
to reach through the veil
to be with each other

the story unfolds
how you want it
if you quantum tunnel
your way through
a dream world
where electrons orbit
outer layers
waiting to be stripped
take hold
of how you traverse
the steps forward
into the unknown

the clarity of love
is only found in science
when one looks
upon a field
seeing all the
electrical charge
stored in the potential energy
of the woman
standing in the tall grass
looking back you

the pace kept brisk
in the muck and mire
of a misty morning trek
two pops in the distance
the gunfire drew masses
of birds to the air
the cacophony raised
my head to the sky
as the birds near me
whispered me a tune
sway in the tall grass
dappled with dew
as the moist ground
squealed under foot
ahead i could hear
the call of seals
luring me
to the warriors
lighthouse

a tonic the way
the moist ground
moves under me
clarity comes
in the silence, always
when your thoughts
connect the footfalls on mud
to free living
the first mission
reclaiming
my soulful connection
for my native state
the fasting trek
of lighthouse treasures
mystery mornings
on Wapato island
shrouded in fog
my thoughts spin poetry
in the ideal
daydream
wry smile
transfixed on nature
i claim silence
listening
to eternity
in the colorful voice
of a river on rock

all these vapor trails
in a turquoise sky
the dance of
two braided locks
of midnight hair
her memory etched
like a poem
swaying in the grass
lining the path i walk
to smile sweet
the daydream memorys
of turquoise silence
moist air lingering
through dappled sunshine
these electrons
connect us
Through charge transfer
when you send your energy
out into the world

these moist droplets
are a lingering reminder
of the failed
quantum communiques
they are messages sent
you never heard
they are failed mechanics
of quantum mathematics
when i didn't quite set
the gain to full intent

lust
nostalgia

quiet your thoughts
to feel your breath
focus
on the sensation
of exhaling
all the negative
you do not need
all the angst
you cannot control
leave it
to dissipate
your entropy

all the days
clinging to
dark nights
of failed quantum
mathematics
i walk
with your smile
remembering
the feeling of
acceptance

alive in the
studio
i hear the
sultry rifts
waft through stratified
layers of smoke
these vibrant
acrylic colors
dance on my toes
like the splatter
of ecstasy
as i throw paint
on a blank canvas
wishing instead
this quantum chemistry
could overpower distant
activation energy
its all these
mathematical communiques
that wish our
outer orbital electrons
would strip each
other bare
in the sultry
night air

in my silence
lived a despair
which one
could not see
only feel
when i slipped
away
it consumed
all the joy
in reverse
until i waded
through
all the lonely
days and nights
of years
to find
the sun
before me
on the cliffs
first light
carried
your love
to me

i wish
the light
cascading
through
the last
of my darkness
could linger
with me

it reminds me
of days
when i felt
your smile
like the freedom
of an eagle
souring high
on thermals
of loss

i lived deep
in melancholy
like a dream
you cannot wake from
it wells up
deep within
till you
thrash about
in the turmoil
of memories
i never shared

i miss
entropic moments
like the sound
of your laugh
in a crowd
lost in the
din of dives
your smile
which shines
like a pulsar
in a dark
night sky
the sound
of your voice
when our pleasure
knew no bounds
i miss
your vibrant
simplicity
the way
you held my hand
with your careful gaze

i clinged
to you
in the
debaucherous
night
when all
the
dives
left me
lonely

i miss
the sound
of my voice
reading words
to you
strung together
deep in my heart
i miss
the feel
of my poems
flowing
through my fingers
as they
trace your skin
the scent
of our pleasure
lingers
in the air
like moist droplets
before saturation

standing on
thirteenth and Burnside
remembering
the horns blaring
people heckling
first kisses
passionate hands
the touch of
your skin
as i stroked
your cheek
before your lips
sparked life
in my toes
standing
on the corner
its raining
now
on my
nostalgia

it is all there
on the surface
all the feelings
hope
sadness
lust
despair
anger
all the tears
fall
like moist droplets
in a desert
disappearing
before anyone
sees
i have no mask
i am still
standing
here
feeling
my
humanity

i woke
bleeding out
these emotions
of honest
expression
no longer filtered
by an unkown
process
i'd cry forever
it seems
if i had no sense
of its affect
on my
spacetime

i realize
in the quiet
there is no
way to quit
if you pause
wait
be mindful
of your thoughts
of your motives
its not failure
or giving up
you are
rethinking
your understanding
altering course
its called
processing slowly
making progress

i listened
to my breath
focussed
on the flow
of electrical
impulses
spurred
by biochemicals
dissolved in solution
i hoped
images would
manifest
the day
you lay
your
head
on my thigh

listen to the birds
who sing
in the wrong
time of year
louder
than normal
the day
of silence
longs for
your vanity
corrupted
your moral center
your greed
it starves
your brain of nutrients
like this
climate reality
starves
humanity's future

i am a hard edge
for the soft soul
a blunt force
trauma
for the abrasive
prick
one way
or another
i will come
for you
either to love
all you show
or to destroy
all your
evil
i claim no
preference
to either
in these dark days
when only a fools hope
keeps you going
in the dire
moments when
evil forces you
to choose
choose kindness
always

the sips of coffee
taste smooth
as they fill my veins
with the elixir
i keep writing
to you as
i place this
love
on the wind
via the water
knowing
you may need
it most
in the coming epoch
in this universe
or an alternative one
some where
in spacetime
you and I
exist
for the
fulfillment
of joy
lust
and the love
we carry
throughout
our adventures

i changed
that which
i despised
yet it did not
satisfy
so i changed
others
to alleviate
my despair
yet it did not
satisfy
this ravenous need
terrorizing me
only the day
darkness consumed
all the light inside
i could see
i must change myself
align
my mind
body
spirit
to be full

the whisper of
your voice
greets me in the
morning sun
like a quantum kiss
on ruby lips
softly brushing
my cheek
do you feel
my smile
light up the room
creating quantum
ripples of
our entanglement
will it unravel
like ruffled white sheets
piled on a bedroom floor
the comfort of
empty heads
with chaotic hair
it's your whispers
i hear
in last light
an invisible quantum link
keeping us entwined

there are moments
where the irony
of existing
weighs on you
like a comedy
you realize
the important pattern
on a rainy afternoon
in late November
the smiles
stretch your skin
swell your heart
like no other
entropic gift
life
forty two
is
unfolding
as a jazz show
of my poetry
spoken each
as a theme
of riffed variations
each time i morph
my melodic cadence

in all the years
i walked
earth
alone
i see you
like me
yet never
have we met
in anything
other than my dreams
all these words
strewn as poems
for you
to read
someday

transcending
rainbows
in the dark

so much for the world
of rainbow butterflies
frolicking in warm sun
it is not a world
of possibility
when your light is
spent
forgotten
a precarious emotional state
of longing mixed depression
seated deep
inside a soul
needing a watering
from you
from me
a reality made
from the warped view
of psychotropics
taken in mass
i awoke this morning
knowing my decisions
we're all wrong
i could never
make amends
to you

infamous kisses
belong to
the corner of
Burnside and Thirteenth
in front of the Annex
as paparazzi clamor
our first embraces
passionate moments
etched in smiles
the debauchery shared
on street corners
in dive bars
drunken sleep sex
eating sushi at Massu
a first date
for epic beginnings
yet i blotted
your eyes
then vanished
like a wraith
running from
my demons

the perfect reality
dissipates dreams
after energy is stripped
by entropic means
this west coast visit
of three boho hippies
layering smoke
to an earthly hymnal
braids of color
dance on my senses
a vintage cherokee
sways fringe aesthetics
wafting pheromonal allure
into the atmosphere
i inhale
her gentle kiss
on my left cheek
as layers of smoke
mix with smiles
lovingly warm
den of laughter
humming conscious
indelibly penned
moments
of Emily Jane

i sit quietly
soaking up
all the notions of fun
my smile etched tightly
on the joy
i keep watching
the sensual
female photographer
kneeling on the bed
the model hovering
as her glide
takes her across
the studio
a form of porn
for artists symphoney
needing fun

the pursuit of pleasure
in the absence of
the collective
good work
for earth
while under
the great peril
of extinction events
you clearly are
on the wrong side
of history
here lays the dichotomy
of modern times
governed by quantum mathematics
the reality of climate change
follows the heretics
rooted in self love
of mystics manifesting
solo realities in isolation
the pursuit of pleasure
in the absence of work
misses the perspective
of self sacrifice
for the greater good
of earthlings

i walk through tall canopies
of ancient forest green
the silent footfalls
on needle paths
carry forward my daydreams
like stallions racing
on an open plain
i wait under a dripping pine
the trees whisper and sway
like i imagine you
in a vintage dress
floating through time
when you twirl
in sunshine
dancing to translate
the emotional landscape
of dripping joy

a steamy mist
wafts up from
a moist folly
we laid bare
all those moons
from now

your pheromones
cling to my cilia
as I inhale
a vain effort
to impress
my memory
of what
love
felt like

the light dances in the window
like glistening shards
of fiery hues
cascading a halo
reflected in your eyes
you smile
a wonderful smile
as i swoon

i crave the fierce
electricity
as your skin
brushes mine
the faint whisper
of pheromones
scented with
love

i am the poetry
of your dream world
manifested
in my distress
a biochemical signature
transfered to form
by the fierce power
of your quantum
messages of love
sprinked throughout
creation
from nothing
at the dawn
of the universe

facing contemplation
in another
wayward poet
an experienced dancer
on the wind
as a sad affair of expectations
pissed down the drain
wasted all the
delicious orgasms
on young ladies
without artistic ways
i see in the eyes of another
the same experience lived
a wayward poet
of the wind
experienced in this sad affair
learned over time
you must give
all your love away
to harness
the excitation inside
to keep the pleasure of our kisses
when carnal ways
come freely
on the days
we write
stories on paper

there is a way
you look at me
through your brown eyes
dark scarlet lips
dripping with the disdain
of a thousand years of pain
your lips pursed
a rye smirk
dancing eyes
my heart swoons
for when you speak
poetess words
from the depth
of a soul
driping
melancholy

as these moist droplets
of sunshine clatter on
electron rich metals
i am the free radical
you seek in the night
to quench your thirst
with dharma
exploration of lovely skin
in a favorable moist folly
of symphonic pleasure
i let biochemicals
run riot over senses
as warm breath
surveys sensitivity
catalogging chemical properties
of pure pheromones
mapping emotional landscapes
of charged love poems
written in the waning hours
of our dreamscape

my first living memory
of this luscious brown curve
led me to a stenciled fish
ornate like a persian
your toes glowed
apocalyptic pink
over an alpine lake
the deep kind you want
to swim in for days
for the health effects
of glacial water
soak up
the exotic scent
of darkness alive with possibilities
there are rainbow colors
in every drop of water
the light of the universe
inhabits these poems written
of the universe
singing of love
from beginning to end

all these words written
on our ancient friends
they speak of a longing
as if it were yours
we know its mine
yet you feel it too
these moist messages
quantum tunnelling to you
as if i could reach out
to caress you
to rest my heart
inside yours
for a few moments respite
feel your blood pumping
kiss your love
like it were my own
the longing of acknowledgment
comes from
lovers liquids passed in time
all these words are written
on ancient friends
for you to read
someday

i believe there is a tomorrow
worth more than today
one where i can gaze upon
your skin like a canvas
see your sacrifice
as a wonderful tapestry
i will jump in
so we may create
redemptive joy
i know only deepening sorrow
from all the things lost before
riding the rapids bareback

be the water now
which flows free
onwards
i am the rock
you crash into
on your journey
we will meet
again and again
until we are miscible
flowing in the eddy
which circles me

i remember the lone tree
as it stood on the horizon
sacred haystacks in the distance
the air cringed with salty stillness
heavy in late afternoon sunshine
you are the perfect stereo isomer
to that ancient tree
as it braves the winds
of an angry coastline
i see resilience in you
the same beautiful
way you carry your history
rooted in love
you are the embodiment
of my words
waiting to be the poems
we fall in love with

i once saw this mushy
pink moon on the horizon
where the ocean waves
shimmer in the fading light
instead of crashing the sand
a pounding
ever steady
emotional tug o' war

sitting in the wood chair
the morning light dances
upon your plush skin
my coffee steams
out over my cup edge
catching some of those light beams
before they dance
upon your lusciousness
i want to kiss your body
till i find a ticklish spot
i want to write my memories
on your inked skin
till i am the memory inside you
filling you with hope
so these stories
of you and i
do not become
the memories of lovers

your voice sings me a song
from a far off land
i smile each time i hear
your melody in my ear
like first light in spring
it realizes all the joy
of new beginnings
when blank pages
are filled with words
telling our story
of transcending barriers
the quantum mathematics
of invisible kite strings
made visible by shared poetry
a story documented on film
when your melody
springs to life
i write words
in the order they need
so you may hear inspiration
for a life of creative exploration
we will adventure through

it feels wonderful
this attention
from you
luscious
exuberant
consumption
you, on the bed
enveloped in white
juxtaposed dark skin
i am smitten by desire
our bodies
communicate love
as you are
this scrumptious poem
waiting for me to write

watching the sun fade
layers of lemon merengue
i wished for more
time with you
more laughter
as if the mere touch
of a lovers hand
fulfills desire
in dangerous times
when the sun
is blotted by
particle agglomeration
from the climate
appocolypse

listen passionately to the wind
it speaks in memory
of a future time we share
quantum state functions
in the mathematics of nonlinear
words juxtaposed upon
supple brown skin
adorned in ink splatter
you are a post modern art event
i crave to explore

when i focus my desire
i can breathe in your pheromones
a soft exhale of essence
i hope will reach you
if my mathematics harmonize
when i close my eyes
to suck in your electrons
can you feel my chest exhale?
our quantum states
across this spacetime
as electrons spin their way
through outer orbitals

i crave the open road
of ever present music
the spirits journey
taking the crossroads
for exploration
waiting for you
so you may take my hand
through the dark matter
of brilliant days
long nights entwined
these adventures
always deepen
the way
i see
the open road
in relation to me
at the crossroads
i'll wait
till my last days
with patience
like a mountain
existing for you
to summit

compositional thoughts
are tough to master
when the sun first arrives
to chase the darkness away
these last few weeks
i sense non linear thoughts
like a radar detects metallics
they speak of your skin
singing to me
of this human leap of faith
i must transcend
to bring us together
the warmth of moments
carried upon the media of life
telling tales as you whispers
i am coming for you
the lover I need
as the love you deserve

these moments when I'm all alone
i listen for your heartbeat
carried by gravity
through spacetime
beating for me
to inspire
the smile you evoke
a deep breath exhaled
in the quiet of the apex
i can feel your lips
throughout my spatial
frame of reference
its a memory
or whim of fancy
to hold tight
in those quiet moments
of our hearts beating

i can feel all of it
flowing through me
the chaos and beauty
an order of magnitude
running faster and faster
with my face
focused west at sunset
your hand on mine
all the hues
caressing your skin
i feel all the memories
we have not shared
like waking dreams
keeping darkness at bay

i hear the humming
voice of love in the distance
the warmth clings to me
moist and sticky
like vibrational electrons
strumming messages of you
outer orbitals fracture
our status quo
moist and sticky
i'm humming now
in your cadence
my pitch flows
along the trajectory
which perfectly aligns
your vibrational frequency
listen closely
you will feel electrons
on nerve endings
this warmth blows
as communications for you
softly on skin
till love hums
along your nerve endings

the tangible light
whispers to the wind
words written in sand
the hue is visceral
like feet in silica particulates
the cold pacific washes
the silence of chaos
all these feels are
screaming outward
waves of electrons
supercharged particles
whose intent is unfulfilled
by the unresolved
hopes and dreams
shared with myself
written in the wind

all the sounds of chaos
smell like desert wildflowers
blooming in the wrong time of year
i see the wish you made
when carbon dioxide
took flight with dandy lion seeds
it is simple
for a lone wolf
like me
to see you
on a hillside
along the open road
only to pass by
in silence

the crash of waves
reigned down like sunshine
i could hear my inner voice
continue with excitement
as smiles flashed
centuries of shared knowledge
the foamy suds of sea salt
rolled away
like dew on a leaf
in the morning

i crave
all that is
you
not
the you
so perfect
but
the you
broken
filtered
be speckled
forgotten
the you
even you find
a mess
this is
what
i crave
everyday

you linger here
in the space between
my hopes and dreams
where all my
wild thoughts reside
these moments
are like a whisper
a song of the ocean
upon the sand
will you hear it
if i ask the wind
to carry it to you

these instant photographs
are visual reminders
of the vibes i miss
in our conversations
as the poetry
currents
take me down
dark stretches
of lonely roads
i look upon nostalgic photographs
to bring me back into the light

the day after an ominous number
foretells the virtues of disaster
when these precarious emotional antics
lead you in all the directions
simultaneously
neurons fire continuously
making the imagery of thought
more like a surrealists nightmare
than a lingering mob
waiting to see if entropy wins

you know the times
when your moments
are epiphanies
wrapped in a
cacophony of fish guts
this bile you drink
is the poison
of the masses
your response
to dark times
dictates something
more extreme
than a disengaged
proletariat

these winds rage on
in the face of mass corruption
like a wayward bear
booking it across a four lane byway
deep in a redwood forest
we can only laugh at this farce
a society lost to the blue light
during a time of unprecedented gadgets
manipulation flows like a river
filled with useless degrees
swollen by the mudflow
created from a clear cut design
in moments like these
remember not to piss in the wind
rather orient your self
so the rage pelts your back
while you look forward
into the untainted wild
of a progressive future
these are the dying days
where we chose to reinvent
or die from the status quo
of incremental change

looking upwards
at a pale blue sky
the bright sun
shines intensely
through photosynthetic leaves
glowing neon green
the clouds dance thinly
with no definition
they pale in contrast
like those nights
which turned to days
in a sea of white covers
it was warm in Paris
so we went to the Alps
the Pyrenees
for a swim in aqua lakes
of melted glacial silt
crisp dips to cool
our lust for life

my story
in the mirror
is vapor
the scenes
like lines
written by entropic tremors
this heart lust runs
epic daydreams
on my delicate emotional psyche
i miss the hedonism
so blatantly wanton
which brought me to you
those nights filled
with whiskey passion
the laughter of your smile
i told anti pious jokes for
these days
flow with the honey
of my melancholy
i carry it deep inside
where it wafts up
to envelope all hope

i sing along to the hue
humming my way free
from entropy's deathly grip
i wish you knew
some things are about timing
more than we khow
if entropy ever wins
in the near term
please know
you and i could have
destroyed time
if i used
my voice
to share with you

i feel it coming soon
for me
like it may
for us all
someday
so says the third law
of thermodynamics

i have always felt
with the love
of a kind woman
we could
rewrite physics
in the form
of some bohemian life
so I could avoid
my entropic death

i crave a moment
of respite
from the way
your electron orbitals
aligned an ill will
the moments desired
are momentum leeches
for you
to show me
what I knew
all along
this ending
is unwell

i wanted to go
to the pow wow
red sister
the quantum tunnel
lost its proton mass
so i lost my way to you
i miss the sway
of your wind enveloping me
when your flapper dress
clings softly
to the vapor barrier
between skin and universe
each puff of smoke
wanders away
a universal mystery
of dark colored twine
wrapped in your pigtails
dancing their way
through my electron orbitals
swift memories i feel
visceral in the moment
as it lingers
softly
on my breath

during audible moments of magic
your intentions must be clear
to throw your might
into this world
the charged particles agglomerate
via brownian motion
until their charge
reaches activation
then its off to execute
what it is you thought
your intentions were
when i am aligned
with all my alternatives
i push out an idea
for the universe
to bring back to me
this episodic day dream
written from deep inside
tied to my core
i dreamed a dream
of you and i
i never held
more than a second
before it evaporated

the faint sunlight whispers through
a moist sky of muddy white
i keep humming a tune of hope
as the eclectic hue of your style
rolls away
electric clouds dripping
this elusive vapor
born from the wind of your sway
i feel the charge transfer hitting me
my synapses fire
joyous light
a precursor to something profound
i taste your scent on my lips
lingering as if you are next to me
reading from your book
the elegant native woman
your boho style
a reflection of simple joy
you bring these charged electrons
to sing to us
of outer orbitals
pressing your hand to my arm
our smiling eyes
linger in these etched moments

standing for a moment
perfectly still
i am engulfed in grey
on all sides
possibilities are limited
welcome to the bottom
a purgatory for mania junkies
it is disorienting my ability
to visualize direction
apathy is without purpose

adrift in a Tullee fog
on a mountain side
back home
this is not
my reality
only the bottom
of a perpetual cycle

i woke up
when the sun
lit the wall
with the eternal
mathematics
of star shine
i could feel
the neutrinos
passing through me
they carried messages
from you
of the harmony
of love
you exhale
with each
breath

in the mornings
when the mist
clings to the hills
i feel your warmth
as first light
touches my skin

will you
kiss me
here
in dappled
moonlight
streaming
starshine
through
ancient
forests
who wink
vast galaxies
above
us

a small group of wildflowers
danced in the morning wild
as the moon crashed
a mighty pacific
into volcanic remnants
the type of cataclysm
life springs from
in the light
of their pastels
glowing from salted air
i hover near the edge
the cliff face
vertical and fierce
as wave after wave
crashed against rock
like I craved
you would
with me

take my hand
to keep
this leisure pace
as we stroll
together
silica pebbles
pushing between
our toes
take my hand
for adventures
of kindness
dripping love
take my hand
so when time
comes calling
for you
in the darkness
i will be there
to adventure
for love

the canvas is blank
until i hear
all my own broad brush strokes
grandiose and worldly
a vast particular vision
of epic stories
elongated
over the sum of time
it takes my dreams
of self
to unfold
as a vivid hallucination

the folds unravel
like a weighted song
of ancient tales
we speak in our sleep
a way to remember
the vision
the ancients gifted us
those who lead the artistic life
lack the quality sleep
to remember details
as we stay up late
get up early
rustle our way
through the night
absorbing the vision
as we can
then opening our heart
to create from it
everyday

i went to the pow wow
on fathers day
like i did as a kid
on mothers day
i could feel
all the love
red sister
the people all smiled
while the drums beat
the heart of ancient ways
their dancing motion
reminded me of leaves
riding the wind
like stallions
of Brownian motion
i swayed for hours
till my eyes
filled with tears
the summer sun
lit us like a spot light
freeing the spirit
of my soul

i keep thinking
as the world unfolds
you are sitting
somewhere
under the same
sunlight
you are standing
with your hair
in the wind
arms outstretched
as you reach
the perfect
stretch
i keep thinking
of yoga in the warm
morning sun
the north central coast
west of the center
your mystic ways
speak strong
as the birds sing
sweetly to me
of you
in all your
glory

i turned north
looking up the beach
clicked the shutter
an instant photograph
of a lovely woman
walking her dog
as she wandered close
i gave her the photograph
handing it to her
with my giant smile
she touched my hand
purposefully
a heartfelt thank you
in her touch
i felt this surge of energy
in that moment
i knew the kindness
of her soul
as she walked on
i watched her sway
my body warm
my smile wide
a thank you
in this wind worn way
i carry her kindness as love

quantum messages
written from
emotional metaphysics
woven into the tapestry
of all my moist follies
those public endeavors
failures and successes
are the changes
of electrons transferred
from me as lessons
abandon the things
which tear me down
the lessons of messaging
survive at all cost
in these dangerous times
choose love
for yourself
for the wayward souls
you meet
along the road

these boho fashionistas
with their artistic glasses
hidden snobbery
their reality
is like everyone else
a comatose mess
of lethargic idiocracy
we need to transcend
a mindful way of living
in harmony to the land
one hundred percent renewable
coupled to emotional metaphysics
the conduit of our future
shared through the voices
of our past
we are the generations
who can transform
humanity's fate

your voice clings
to stratified air
like the scent
of limp lillies fading
into summer light
they left their essence
in the height of spring
just a vestige
of our love in color
as these are the days
we bleed out
the bile of modern ways
releasing the pooled toxins
which siphon our vitality
from our daily life

your sense
of non preparedness
is strongest
when you face
your existential strife
head on
with forward momentum
resulting from choices
made with conscious
thoughts
stopping all the chaos
dead in its tracks
so you can listen
to the joyful silence

the sensationalism
of your selfishness
as a tool to promote
a twisted art form
perverse in its exploits
of both photographer and model
perverse in its ability
to drain you of your sexuality
all that juicy energy
ends up in the photograph
with nothing left
for you to carry forward
into your personal life

listen to the hum
of your eros
its cadence
you can hear
over the din
of your existence

i whisper
all my pretty words
into the wind
they are the seeds
of hope
which grow in the sun
so it will bathe you
with its vital energy
when the moist follies
come to stay awhile

take me
the way i dream
after the sun sets
its rays of hope
after you whisper
all the pretty words
to make me swoon

the simplicity sought
is driven by desire
to end the conflict
of internal despair
forged in the cataclysm
of busted dreams
i crave the washed
feelings
of forgiving failures
when you are stripped bare
there is no hiding
from your self

say goodbye
to whatever
you wake up without
say goodbye
to whatever
you can muster
to live without
just drop them
erase them
burn
or do
whatever
you need
to lighten
the load

i whispered your name
in my head
to the self
who hears it
knows of you
it's the simple perspective
where audible exclamations
equal joyous smiles
the way ink on paper
laid without desperation
of a lifelong singularity
leads to powerful
ways of breathing
life into self

all these years
writing beautiful
love poems
to a mythical
woman
who may only
exist
in a parallel
spacetime

i dream of you
in my private time
smiling as
you squirm
each time i kiss you
these brazen daydreams
wonder what your skin says
when caressed often
daydreams are time travel
hidden behind a quantum threshold
of improbable mathematics
may we be
more than messages
riding the light
between your spacetime
and mine

in all these visions
i keep dreaming
of skin on thigh
brushed soft
by my fingertips
stoking
favors
till hues
dance like stars
in our eyes

when i finally
fixed upon your eyes
these muddled pale
green amber eyes
they permeate me
with a piercing longing
all the feelings
comforting sadness
lingering in me
like the warmth of a blanket

i quit day dreaming
blind hope
so long ago
yet through strands
of glistening hair
your luminous glow
emanates from the smile
in eyes
where hope resides

i listen to waves
crash the shore
as i wish
you would
on me
feeling the moist
bitter sea salt
carry the force
of the moons
pull on the earth
white capped
velocity
bravely written
as shear existence
over millenia

i wanted a visceral way
to crash into you
to awake my desires
so passion
of a paramour
would destroy
the apathy
currently eating
my hope
like a greedy pig
sucking life from
all the trans isomers
i lost

the late April light
rains down
illuminating hues
of hipster minimalism
as postscript analytical

she was all forms of gnarly
when she boldly asked me to coffee
an instant connection
through gray wisps
we carry our experience
into those first dynamic voices
as the electric charged clouds
bristled with the buzz
of first touches
rainbows sprouted from nowhere
leaping out in front of us
all that electric potential
communicating via water
a message of love
unconditional in its charge transfer
moist golden clouds
of milky yellow hue
surrounded by darkening storms
we're an oasis of respite
which spawned three rainbows
after the onset
of your skin on mine

morning light fills the room
with love projected throughout
i smile at the feeling
of your skin on mine
like its our reality
today,
as the light
dances for you
through all the distant
starshine you bask in
while my smile floods
a joyful hope
of my love
riding the light
to you
in morning prayer

i claim your body
a masterpiece of art
the way your brown skin
lures my eyes
to seek you
the way your ink
softly contrasts
the region of skin
i crave exploring
like all masterpieces
i wish to absorb
its love
by basking
in your presence

sitting with my feet
out in front
i take the full dose
to cure
all the love anguish
of poison feelings
as if no choices are written
in the setting sun
all my years
living like this
where no one sees me
blowing in the wind
these two shadows
of light silhouette
i swallowed
the full dose
squared
a cure for
quantum feels
waiting on the sun
to bathe
these dances
written in the dark

i cling
to first light
sunrise moments
as a weight
keeps me
from rising up
to receive
your messages
written on
first light

the grey
cool
early summer
mornings
whisper words
you never
spoke
on days
we never
met

i sometimes pour
two cups
of black coffee
in artists mugs
made in Zion
i set yours
next to the
boho swing
so i may
see the steam
waft up
where your skin
should be

your careless
muddled heart
lead me
to resign dignity
as biochemicals
rape my grey matter
my epic brain
fighting ego
over a careless heart
to selfish
to give all
my love away

i am the poet
who projects you
into others
despite you being
my imagination
i wonder
if the breath
i inhaled
with a whistle
is recognition
of your expressions
in others
its why
i am
smitten
by smiles
written on the wind

the grip
of a twisted nature
still a force
not forgotten
its strength wanes
in the lagging
light
of
growing
old

the universe's
theory
coded

the foam floats
a murky amber
a loss of purity
its State function
mathematics
once complex
now
a linear squares
wet dream
solved with basic
first principles

i am like a pendulum
when forcibly slowed down
i stall out
looking for a kick start
a way to propel this mania
back onto a ripe trajectory

places like the Neskowin
where i stand listening
to the power of ocean beats
are sacred
to those who came
before me

the rush of biochemicals
are simple charge
transfer
messages
are a ferry
floating the bay
with a contagious wind
i could share
with you

this feels like the final days
when all darkness reigns down
if we're to go down
then let this evening
be how we remember
our humanity
craving all the skin on skin
spent in carnal embrace
a champagne reality
you feel
before the thaw
our self regulating poles
should build a climate
of love and balance

the pounding
of waves onshore
call to me
to get on the road
find my uncertain
time
of mysterious smiles
waiting like moist droplets
on the wind

these emotions
run wild in me
like singularities
of dark matter
an atomic aftermath
of outer orbitals
electrons
stripped clean
of the atom of origin
its like when you
kissed my cheek
with the wind
of a thousand generations
i could see
a love
in the days
ahead

demons of my night
entropic dances
i will always lose
the third law
dictates
manic ends
on top
of the world
till you stare up
from the gutter

age creeps up on me
like brownian motion
in a vapor trail
all wrapped
in a chemical soup
where
pheromones
latch onto
receptor fields
in suppression
feedback loops
biochemistry
cannot curtail

this longing is not for
the dreams of my youth
or the love
never felt
this longing is for
simplicity of connection
which embraces love
projected through nebula's
of mystical star dust

i say
do not fall hard
for forever
with me
is a long fight
for emotions
to balance

this moment is crushing
the weight of disease
destroying your spirit
in a deep darkness
bent on eating
your hope
eventually it consumes
all opportunity
leaving a vacant hole
for depression to fill
a singularity in space
consuming everything
in the universe
held dear

we are the leaders
those who see
the way
before all others
we are who
our ancestors hoped
we would be
now is the time
we transform all others
so we may
cleanse the way
for earths rebirth
without the plague
of capitalistic consumerism

a deep warmth
permeated
along all my
nerve endings
as the pitocin
concentrations
grew
you held firm
our embrace
so i inhaled
all your
pheromones
till my smile
supercharged

shades of isolated grey matter
sink into an inertial mess
of visceral worlds
spoken in the silence
of unstructured thought
this is the death
i have kept
at bay
for all the years
i hoped
love would return

the mastery of chaos
comes from an infinite
application of energy
the resultant
net order
is a feat mildly witnessed
on a universal scale
the creative force
of quantum messaging
through abstract art
with any medium necessary
it becomes a means
of enlightenment
the decoded messages
sent into existence
at the time of the big bang
all these quantum messages
our ancestors formed
from star shine
as they lay under
chaotic abstracts
i now throw paint at

you are the answer
to the universal question
on this rotation
around the sun
here is your gift
you wished for
the chaos
of your fight
the universe became
your expression of art

the moon rides full
on the longest night
it rises in the east
like the sun
a pale beacon
lighting the sky
for celebration
of you and I
dancing wild
naked
in the brisk
winter air
a celebration
of love
to raise the
new moon
on the longest
night of the year

own the mystery
you are an entropic
particulate of light
born from universal creation
in the mathematics
of spacetime
on this solstice
of the shortest day and
the darkest night
longest of this trip
around the sun
celebrate
the new growth
from previous inspection
accept the requirement
for mindful introspection
own the mystery
to allow the experience
of feeling joy
again

all the years
have left
the scent of life
experienced
in solo
epic adventures
i am the
spoken word
written in events
played out over time
a ball of hydrogen
burning in a vacuum
bringing the light
of many moons
to me
i have learned
the transient
mathematics
of a native tongue
only to miss out
on the permanence
of deep roots

time is nonlinear mathematics
while perception
is a linear hodgepodge
of cartesian coordinates
four dimensional spacetime
in the silence vacuum
of a singularity
craving the nostalgia
of tracing messages
of love
on your skin

the scent of surreal
filled the nostrils
with the disdain
of all my failed
attempts to launch
it stank up
all the views
i expressed
until i sat
in silence

the shine of hope
burned hotter
than our sun
like the warm splash
of waves on silica
as the morning
arose with the
moist sorrows
of broken mathematics
it was like watching
a puddle of water
in the desert
evaporate
the final vanishing act
of hope for a man
under duress

i cling to this outer orbital
like a quantized spiral
of a bald eagle in flight
it is the dream of a romantic
to tunnel through
spacetime
anywhere in this universe
just to
hold your hand

craving the bubble
of you and i
quantum
math predicts
when we touch
worlds collide
like two black holes
in an ancient nebula
you lean in for a kiss
the sensation works
like pheromones and flowers
our fragrance an aphrodisiac
of quantized states
lingering
in each touch
i wonder
if this is perfection
peacefully sitting here
your body flush with mine
every electron
on your inked skin
tastes like ice cream
the scrumptious delight
of craving your scent
like a honeybee
desires a flower
it is these quantum states
colliding in moments
spoken in the nights
spent in each others arms

the vitamin light
dapples and dances
through a giant vacuum
the charge transfer
can bridge millennia
if we focus our intent
on the water
as thousands of generations
have safely navigated till now
we must listen to their spirit
protect the sacred essence
of our existence
it is a universal
truth
fundamentally rooted
in a mindful balance
with mother earth

i see the mist fall like a blanket
upon the visual landscape
this time our history
is a perversion beyond hope
if i linger
for a breath or two
will i even see
the progressive path forward
as this mist seeps deep
into the landscape i am

electrons sit idly
locked in inner orbitals
this theory of quantum love
a bridge we built
so long ago
to communicate pheromones
across light years
my truth weighs
heavier than a gram
or the scent
of desert rain
coupled to a moist folly
one of us is remiss
to see stable bridges
filled with mathematics
which allow my electrons
to swim in desert streams
till the future
is our story
written in the stars

in the time
when the sun sags
some of us reinvent
the meaning of self
while others rise up
to be counted
among those who claim
nothing but the stewardship
of our Mother Earth

these singularities
expand at a rate
far outpaced by the
compression i felt
moments before
your lips lay
on my skin
the spring board effect
is rather like a vapor expansion
of a compressed gas
it expands freely
running free
like stallion feelings
on wanderlust

these letters are folded
like a three dimensional enzyme
all the receptor sites
nestled near the hydrogen bonds
they are my way
to quantum message you
these words layered
by charge transfer synapses
firing an orderly poem
i wrote to you
in psychotropic smoke signals
quantum tunnelling through
all of spacetime

the dipole of moisture
sits ideally
in its hydrophobic state
just a raindrop
waiting for absorption
to absolve its sins

the melodies i keep hearing
are more like a story
the birds can understand
like flying south for the winter
a mass exodus of culture
seeking a folklife
creative living
on her own
in the middle of no where
longing
craving
to live honestly
amongst the natural world
as our brothers and sisters
of old did
their sacred path
a homage to connect us
to the source of our love
i see rainbow colors
in all the liquid sunshine
as the time is here
when we must all
turn our backs
on the blue light
and trek into the wild
to enrich our love

this temptation i feel
rising up like the tide
fits my mood
like flowers in June
i want to run free
on an adventure
through all spacetime
till i find you
swaying in the wind
looking out over golden hills
lusting after the never-ending blue
of sea salt dissolution
bound to the dihydrogen oxide
lapping on silica
i am three steps from the door
thinking of your pigtails
dancing their way across the horizon
this dream is a road trip away
from an epic tale
for our surreal age

kindness is your moisture
like at twilight
when the birds sing
a tune of the wind
whiping silently
i do all these psychotropics
to supercharge my particles
allowing me to tunnel
all the places i desire
you and i
to occupy
i write these electrons like atoms
with all their outer orbitals filled
in hope of memories
sharing twilight
my visual cortex salivates
for your native sway
your favorite vintage dress
dark pigtails dangling
the vapor trails in orien's belt
as your aura seeps into me
our combinatorial mathematics
are the mechanics of quantum love

i long for the sound of native flutes
the whistle of birds
singing a wondrous tune
i know you would be swaying
if you were here
telling me a story
of your grandeur
as the sway of the leaves
rustle a moist spice scent
the incense of herb burns
temperature gradients
between you and i
so our pheromones travel
to one another
at the speed of light

i am on the road of atonement
for my mother earth
who i have wronged whilst doing right
sometimes i feel blessed
sometimes cursed
this matter a whim
of a child
who chases butterflies today
like he did as a child
to lay out by a stream
brownian clouds stratified
dreaming big
of where the eagles
fly over crashing waves
wearing down the rocks
this passage of time knows
you are what i crave
on the wind

this absorption of audible mass
says the quantum math
is simple reminders for
when the wind naps
the flowers are contented
when the bees come
for pollen to make honey
this sweet entropic state
is why i long for you
to sway your hips
hand dancing
this melancholy i carry
i see
your dance
a brownian sway
of lovely words
waiting for the flourish
of a kiss

i will keep these promises
as scraps of paper
for the wind to motion
so you will forget
how to find
the mist of my
quantum tunneling
i want to chase you
to outrun my nefarious entropy
so i feel the love
for mother earth
herself a dance
in the wind
her words
the suns embrace

these bonds are ionic
with all the ease
to dissolve a salt
i am the example
of knowing a life
lived as a target
entropy is coming for me
fast and hard
like a death sentence
you cannot avoid
these bonds dissolve easy
the elections stripping
my outer orbitals
clinging tightly
to the interest
i wish you had in me
i am the example
of knowing eventually
entropy wins
due to the mathematics
of the third law

the early morning hours when i wake
are a dark silence of me
the plans in my sensations
race like electrons
charge loading synapses
until a plethora of visuals
hone the reward
dark warm elixir of psychotropics
the early morning hours
as the sun rises with me
bliss an echo
of my memory of you
doing yoga on the floor
face to face with smiles
puffing my elixir
soaking up all of you
the stoic smiles
of sensual movements
acid etched electrons
charge loading
as grey matter explodes
a rush of pheromones
then the light comes
brilliant and aware

in the quiet moments
between thoughts
all the electrons
pool together
for a microsecond
on your arms
wrapped
around me
i can chart my
endorphins
as they raise
my spirit

charged electrons
spin in outer orbitals
like boho girls
dancing on the beach
in the last rays
of sunset
when your heart
leaps the most
to express
the mathematics
of loving her

you are a powerful
remnant of a time
when the universe
became
from nothing
you have
the power
to create
from nothing

the water flows
in Eddys
of partial algorithms
one could discern
by watching
if not for the
mesmerizing effect
of reflections

it was silent
a moment
as my pace
reached
equilibrium
then the wind
then the birds
a wry smile
creeping again
to rise up
feel hope
opportunities
to reflect
the aspirations
of your dreams
as reality
our immortality
is measured
in what we
leave behind

the tune is a rusted blip
squeaking its way
along a concrete path
these river stones
lay beneath my feet
a tale of redemption
waiting to be written
epic letters
strewn forth
into a sea
of words
laid bare
on blank pages

just look at the flowers
warm and colorful
for a moment
i can dream
for the instant
i can breathe
then overwhelming
sadness rushes up
engulfing all of me
as flowers sway
like they are laughing
at the wind
for fluffing their dance
as daily routine

sitting in Zion
listening to a bird
serenade me
all this love
for the beautiful places
Mother Earth has shown me
sitting here
with incense burning
i think of your
bohemian vibe
another bird joins
the serenade
of earth
as we should sing
along

sipping this cafe'
in the warmth
of Utah sun
the early mornings
of Zion National Park
are remarkable
for the bustle of birds
singing their songs
the hustle of lizards
lurking about
as they grapple for
the warmest spot
in the sun
the wind whips up
a thermal breeze
to toss my hair
as natures stylist

listen to my heart
it sounds of nature
the divine
connection of my thoughts
a first impression
of a peach introduced
my faith
forty years the primer
to prepare
for the final
twenty five

know
without
revel

the linearity of time
is a fallacy of shallow thinkers
who cannot fathom
the coordinates of spacetime
a four dimensional view
curved in nature
a concept known
to a few mindful folks
whose heart aligns
with ancient ways
mindful humans have
the concept of mathematics
solved with the means
to transcend
the nature of spacetime
by changing reality
we time travel
transcending
all four dimensions
sensing our connection
to each universe

the faded Sienna
burnt by its exposure
to life
the tarnish of oxidation
is a permanent layer
of chemical bonds
which grow like calluses
etched over skin
it will all fall away
when calm reflection
revitalizes core essentials
shedding old skin
for a newly divine way
the perceived permanence
of a covalent bond
is an infinite figment
of a marginally precise reality

the climate
of a collected reality
weeps like a window
in a moist environment
its a reminder
of the fragility
of a cycle
on the verge
of collapse

i would read
all the words
i could pen
if all this
advanced
quantum
mathematics
could bridge
the spacetime
divide
set before us

the sound of the waves
crashing into Ruby
like all the days
we walked the earth
a constant
of ancestral wisdom
wrapped
in modern angst

a bleeding of the lines
like all my neural networks
remapping themselves
when the chemical channels
fire seemingly at once
this fabric rewoven
as water molecules
realign their electron's
outer orbitals
shaped by the intent
of mindful beings
the positive
trajectory of reality
we must reconcile
from a shared narrative

listen to the sound
of rustling leaves
it tells you
which way
the wind blows
go opposite
to find adventure
listen to the sound
of footfalls on snow
it tells you
of the silence
you need from solitude
to heal yourself
listen to the birds
sing to you
their song of hope
for the love inside
to be unleashed
for all

you play with powerful forces
when you communicate
experimentally
the quantum chemistry
of kite strings
invisible connections
throughout spacetime
these forces malleable
in the unified theory
of an expansive mind
focus your quiet
in the grey matter
so your outgoing energy
feels of love
quantized viscerally
on moist droplets
of light

a molecular wave
engulfed my neurotransmitters
as her pheromones
saturated receptors
for a microsecond
i feel love
permeating my membranes
this blissful lust
drew a smile on her body
as a molecular wave
of carnal desire
engulfed my energy
all the quantization
of my pheromone response
sought to navigate
her neural chemical receptors
in the moon light

the smile plastered
to my visage
is a massive influx
of psychotropic chemicals
being pumped through
my blood
to ancient receptors
in my brain
introductions of joy
bioengineered to produce
the likelihood
of our linear existence
in this soulless time

bright yellow waves
mixed with orange red
float effortlessly upon
a dark blue sky
its the time
of the sagging sun
when your sentimentality
changes its tune

the hope in quantum mathematics
is the understanding
it brings
to an invisible kite string
connecting you with me
all the moments
my minds eye
shows me
you dancing
barefoot
dress in the wind
twirling wildly free
they are memories
from the centered me
i seek
alternatively

the poppy when plucked
from the ground
cares only to get
you high
in the afterlife
its whimsy
is floating free
upon the light

a lesson you believe
may hope bring
the wind as whimsy
as physics leads math
to quintessential beliefs
your voice existed
somewhere in a visceral alternative
your femme declaration
rustled the leaves
of knowing without reveling
the part of me
no one clings too
in dark moments
of inertial displacement
where the mathematics
for quantized reality
produces a distant tunnel
between you and i

sensing the vibrations
of sentient beings
i listen to the waves
rattle the river rock
it percolates the Rialto
in honor of the earth
all my ancestors
before me
protected
i hear their wisdom
whispered in the mist
the wind carries
them into the world
where saturation
rains them out

i see the arc
of life
quarter arched roads
traversed in a
ping pong ball
of emotions
every nerve
bundle receiving
all the consequences
of visceral signals
the actions
of a dulled heart
years into apathy
it's embers smolder
in the heat
of climate change
living in the desert
during your influential years
the singed smell
of these burning arcs
all the traversed roads
i waited
for you on

words are false
when actions
reflect opposites
the people are
fractured
by this

be kind to yourself
i am counting on you
i need you
now more than ever
i want you
to thrive
i am sorry
my good nature
let you down
again
when i know
you need me
to lift you up
be kind to yourself
you are worth
all of it

for you, not them
there will be moments
of unbelievable bliss
where the wonders
of the universe
are revealed to us
there will be moments
where we only
see dark chaos
entropy grappling
for our chi
love is a choice
you must reaffirm
in the present
if equality
is the daily act
of balance
i choose
love over darkness
i choose the hope
of light
which travelled to us
for all the days
we walk side by side

the years stretched my defenses
expanded my weariness
yet led me to the opening salvo
which allowed your vibrant entrance
of glowing molten light
you are air to my fire
when we adventure

the years taught me
how to see
the way to love
as your smile radiantly
guides those somber days
stretched thin by entropy
when all the longing
is for warm sunshine daydreams

visceral is this craving if unquenched
like savage rampaging emotions
pillaging wayward through
the dark night of my days
stumbling upon shameful steps
towards first light

when i lay my head
on your shoulder blade
there is a freckle
it is a special
part of you
like the way
your lips look
in certain light
it entertains my gentle
kiss on your neck
tracing the edges of your ink
resting on your contoured bliss
i feel the beat
of your heart
synced to mine
when you kiss me back
my hand
slides
into yours

under warm sheets
i long to feel
the grit of your skin
as you wake me
with your love

it made me pant
exhausted
in a moment frozen
i smiled
ear to ear
to help ease
my breath

i do not desire
to consume you
rather seek
to replenish
cherish
the very
essence
of you
i come here
on my journey
seeing you
in my peripherals
i caught a glimpse
of the depth
you carry
in your eyes
those mannerisms
of our history
reflect upon our care
for those that need us

i cling to the insatiable taste
of you on my lips
the high desert in spring
with all the wild flowers blooming
i find my propensity
to meander in the sunshine of thought
till i can smell you on all
the molecules i inhale
your pheromone signature
smells of first rain in the desert
all the masks of your womanhood
a craving that is brand new
i lick my fingers again
as i look into the sky
your soft round smirk greats me
as my molecules dance with yours
your pheromone signature
tastes like words pouring on paper
uttered by our voices in the future
as we chase an insatiable desert spiring

my skin hums when i feel
the friction of our breath
sucking the oxygen from the air
i explore all the hues
inked on your skin
this poetry between us
is a blank canvas of exploration
like how your summer dress
of flowers and feathers
would slip off in the twilight
a tapestry of art i would explore
with brushstrokes traversing
all of your dreams
writhing sensations
which unleash all
your joy
the hum of ecstasy
in faded light
your erect nipples
feel the vibrance
flowing through me
as i whisper
the universe's love
for us

the morning after our torid lust
i could feel you in my blood stream
smell you on my fingers
your musk made me salivate
for the pursuit of your insatiable craving
for the words on my lips
the way we moved in the night
a great mass of human love
sacred in our connection
we are the present
gift from the divine
in dangerous times
when hope needs
a breeding ground
to incubate love
so we may infuse the water with it
for when the northwest rains
our love is a quantum event
rooted in a poetess
a perfect morning paramour

woke to the sound
of rain on metal
falling like communiques
i hope one is from you
so i may inhale you
desperately missing
the endorphin fix
pumping my brain
full of dopamine
open the deluge
of touch
anticipating sparks
flying
i am a honeybee
searching for a flower
to pollenate
i seek your kiss
from pale ruby lips
which taste of
high dessert
in spring
a sweet parched salt laden kisses
filled with the emotions
of an existence
tempted to love
your comfort
when we are away

i wanted a woman
with a hairy bush
ink on her skin
the living art of a poetess
who could weave words
that make me swoon
yet much of my life
i caught turmoil
some heartache
grieving
for things i lost
cheaply along the way
i just wanted to love
all of you who needed it
until you drank your fill
all my life i have sent
these quantum messages
of myself into the universe
seeking the ones
who keep coming around
impossible entropic dreams
i dreamed alone
when the universe
listened silently

i see you standing against the sill
your dress covers half your thighs
the light shown perfectly
on your bronze legs
the ink lit neon
places my kisses there
to ravage you
in mathematical views
of lovesick intoxication
smitten by murky depths
a mirror of my reality
that night as the moon lay waste
to our poetic romance
these battling words
are stories of the times
we stopped along the road
to take a dip in the stream
i kissed your lips first
before hands gripped love
letting juices drip
as bodies collided
our intent to relinquish
the story as it was written

i remember what you tasted of
the night we returned
from the hot spring
it was the sweetest cedar
i licked your cheek
to make you smile
it always felt good
to stand behind you
let you shine
the friction freed our poetry
so others could read
how we loved

walking in march air
in the southern hemisphere
is a sticky moist soup
of relaxed life
so easy to be refreshed
your naked body
glistening smiles at me
the beautiful light
reflecting on you
this delicious kiss
of our wondrous life

i want to feel your warm skin
as i drift to sleep
sticky from delight
i will dream sweet dreams
of love making as art
in the mornings
soft light
daybreak on
your skin
a sensation of arousal
with all the pleasure
our creativity brings

i love this future memory of you
as it carries me to a smile
every time i anticipate it
like a shot of endorphins
in sodium channels
of charge transfers
waiting with potential
like our kisses
which explode delight
when my neurons fire

its not nefarious
to share this life
with you
our existence is worth
all the joy reaped
after plowing
through the muck
of the pain we carry
the river stone
walking paths
of mystical frequencies
fired by neurons
in grey matter folds
we reaped from life

i have been on walkabout
for seventeen years
playing whiskey songs
in all the dive bars
i could find
always chasing
those rye dames
down dark holes
you'd never fail to find
secular debauchery in

i longed for you
to love me for pleasure
all day all night
we confide
in love
always forever
it carried me
through nocturnal hallucinations
of quantized mathematics
with ancestral wisdom
loving you
always forever

when i get lonely
there are blank pages
i can fill with dreams
waking fantasies
to quench
a desire unfulfilled
till i see the waning light
cascade upon your brown skin
glistening reflections
of all the wavelengths
anticipated
the first breath
inhaled
the first touch
of pheromone induced luxury
the luscious scent
on your skin
a cure for lonely feelings
which ravage
a poet in the night

i love to daydream
of all the moments
you looked
in my eyes
with love
i dream these waking dreams
so i may remember
the quantum mathematics
which bring me to you
for all this imagination
is wasted on the selfish
who never endeavor to desire
these backroads
of the spirit
walking
till the day
i recognize you
from my dreams

the anticipation is in the drive
to consume words
so they speak my heart
i slept longingly
for a day
to feel your skin
as inhaled
biochemical
signatures
this fire burns
for the dopamine
you unleash

there is such a clear
distinction
in the moments inhaled
deliberately
sending my love
to you
it's intoxicating
all the
euphoric feelings
of thermal connection
invisible kite strings
of rotational inertia
riding on vibrational waves
of dihydrogen monoxide
if focussed
i can almost see
the light shed grace
on your face
bathing you in
starlight

it is impossible to describe
the inalienable outcome
of mania
entropy always wins
with a high probability
i will take my own life
in a moment
i cannot reconcile
the emotionally charged
landscape of a melancholy
mixed state
through all the years
of constant tears
uncontrolled days
no one saw

always wondering
is today the end

this crush i have
for your green eyes
engulfed in dark hair
has carried with me
through the years
its contrast is beautifully
juxtaposed with my fetish
for your ink
on tan skin
highlighted by
wine laced lips
a lit cig dangling
your sassy overtures
spotted with raunchy humor
which drew me in
like a moist morning fog
ripe with a blanket mentality
it's your smile i dream
will someday out weigh
the sorrow written
in your eyes
this crush i carry
is a refreshing reminder
i am just as broken too
with sad eyes hidden
behind blue filters

i tire of these patterns
on my atypical tuesdays
i can see my reflection
in the may dappled windows
as light sits heavy
with all the sparkle
of strippers and unicorns
on a saturday night

my grip feels loose
when it should be tight
i cannot see through
the moisture in my eyes
entropy is winning
this war for my soul

my heart aches with sadness
so long i loose
when i think i'm winning
it will end really soon
i fear

if the sun refuses
to shine
as the cold inside
takes root
till darkness swims
in tearfilled wells
through the blur
entropy laughs
for the life
it sucks
away

the days flow
with a cadence of you
one born in a memory
from a shared reality
our quantized communiques
carry around the universe
like they are the fabric
of a secret
world where we can be
in this parallel verse

the beautiful songs of you
it is your grey matter
which enticed me the most
it opens the window to your soul
where all the joy and sadness resides
this is where I belong
in the depths
where the words
ignite passion
for dirty foreplay
to satisfy
our primal lust

listen to the sound of rain on metal
you can hear the voices
from quantum messages
left over a thousand generations
i hear them whisper your name
i hear them whisper
of tales told
in your grandmother's voice

the fire burned this warmth
a heat in the night
as i lay basking naked
in the sliver moonlight
surrounded by stars
with wavelengths of light
invading me
i masturbated with the intent
of devouring your
insatiable poetess

i walk out in the rain
hoping the visceral
will meet my face
in the way i imagine
your hand feels
on my cheek
i inhale deeply
as moisture clings to my cilia
bathing my cells
in the love
you send me daily

this melancholy clings
like wet hair on a dog
its salve are remnants
of a moist folly so long ago
it sings to me in the light of day
the deep dark nights
are like a wraith of sadness
hell bent on sucking
all the joy i held tightly
in the crystalline structure
of my water molecules
no one sees this sadness in me
in the lonely nights
of all my days
when i linger in solitude
even in a crowd
they cannot fathom
the depth of this darkness
residing inside all my cells
as interstitial memories
of some trauma
i experienced in a past life
in my ancestors life
i am the manifestation
of memories and experiences
woven
into the fabric
of my DNA
this melancholy clings to me
like a memory

the monuments stood like
pillars to remind us
we are small
yet mighty
in the distance
i see you
fierce in the periphery
this murky mass of love
a seed of something ancient
with wisdom oozing grace
you rock your mocks
dancing in the moonlight
after these desert sentinels
wished for something like
time to remind us to nurture
the earth and each other

the final rays of sunlight
reflected off the sound surface
the sky reaches out
as far on the horizon
as cloud droplets
agglomerate around
particles
of love
i feel your hand take mine
as the last light says goodbye
to this water communique
conveying the beautiful
colors of a shared sunset
the blue pastels reflect
all the trauma left
from persisting
onwards

i try to smile but it comes out a grimace
through gritted teeth with clenched lips
i speak to the biochemistry
as if it already has not failed me
a hundred times over
yet i am here
because i fail in the strength
to control entropy
so it does not run riot
on my biochemistry

being in the know on self
puts you in the improbable position
of self inflicted wounds
when you can only choose
self aware versus thin veiled lies
one caries hope
the other your destruction
one is right
one is conformist
all i crave is lost to me
knowing who i am though
knowing there is no thigh
to rest my head upon
so tomorrow brings
the same anguish
as the sadness of today
the despair of yesterday

i follow the arc of nonlinear affairs
like they are eddies in the wind
for as long as i have known
there is a way to find yourself
a golden ticket in the
dark night of your days
forget how time ticks for us all
for the mathematics of love we seek
is written from the light
of your lovers eyes

footsteps crunch
like weak walking sticks
worn by years
and nature
i cling to each
inhalation
like i can taste
each smell
as if
it were you

the emerald rogue
embraces
the flow of eddies
you can be the rock
shaped smooth
or you can be
the water molecules
flowing free
like gravity

i write for you
all the pretty words
no one wanted
me to say
the pen lays ink
like stars in the night
a mystical light
you smell
my hue
simple blue words
i write
for you
so you may
hear
what no one else
has before
though while
i create
a dream of you
twirling away
the freedom
to run
wild

i exhaled all the emotions
written from the depths
to dance upon the page
i wished
for only my hope
to pass through me
one more time
so i could
dream
again
of this belief in a you
whose head rests
upon my thigh
stroking
bare skin
bioreceptors
are neural pathways
of murals painted
on skin
i'd love
to write on
all the words
for you to swoon after
if you'd let me
pass through the gate
daily
for a visit
between
us two

i wanted to feel it
the deep visceral
longing
which comes only
from
the touch
of a paramour
who has lived
stories written
in the wrinkles
of time
i wanted you
to touch
those pained places
in me
so the heart
could match
this longing

the brush of light stung
like a deep inhale
of frigid air
the kind that burns
before it warms you
i wanted to inhale
your scent
deep into my soul
where your pheromones
would ignite
the words
on a page
we cling too
like the memories
of fingertips
brushing follicles
in moist excitement
if i whispered now
in your ear
would you smile
a golden hue

the birds keep singing to me
the day is waiting
they tell me to rise up from this slumber
i do not want to change
my biochemical state
for laying here i can still
drift off to dreamland
where you are able to touch me
if i rise up to greet these birds
who sing to me of a new day
i fear you will disappear
from the favored
feelings
i have of you
loving me